Paper: The Dirt Roads Crossing the Information Highway

The Business Case for Electronic Records

Patricia Beelby
Marcel Roy

Park Publishing Inc.
Sherwood Park, Alberta, Canada

Paper Trails:
The Dirt Roads Crossing the Information Highway
The Business Case for Electronic Records

Patricia Beelby and Marcel Roy

Published by:
Park Publishing Inc.
212, 10 Chippewa Road
Sherwood Park, AB T8A 3Y1

ISBN 0-9736239-1-8
Printed in Canada
Beelby, Patricia and Roy, Marcel
Paper Trails: The Dirt Roads Crossing the Information Highway
Includes bibliographical references

What Others Are Saying

"If organizations that I've worked with had managed their records as laid out in this book, they might have paid a lot less in legal fees. This book presents a diligent approach to managing records that can assist organizations in meeting their legal obligations."

James T. Swanson BASc., LLB, MBA
Burnet, Duckworth & Palmer Law Firm

Lots of good stuff captured in 93 short pages. The approach used here in Geneva at this UN agency does coincide with several of your key points. We are still a distance from paper as transitory, but that is certainly the direction we are going. And the emphasis on responsibility and accountability is dead on centre.

Lee MacDonald
Archivist of the UN Refugee Agency in Geneva and the former Assistant National Archivist of Canada.

The many stories and examples made the book very readable and accessible. It led me through the very complex area of document management and presented a step by step guide to identifying information management problems and implementing solutions. I particularly appreciated the insight that having an information management strategy will provide corporate peace of mind as well as a rapid return on investment.

Dean Frey, Librarian

An excellent read! A very well-written, wise, thought-provoking and comprehensive guide for busy people who recognize the need for taking both a strategic and practical approach to managing the massive amounts of information in their organizations."

Sid Ridgley, CSP, MBA, co-author "Transformational Leadership"

"Paper Trails from the creative, yet practical minds of Patricia Beelby and Marcel Roy is a must read for any 21st century leading edge organization. They have captured the challenge of focusing our efforts on systemizing how we deal with information to allow us to leverage our energies on more productive parts of our business environments. Well done!"

Bob 'Idea Man' Hooey, Business Success Coach, Speaker Author, "A Legacy of Leadership" and "Creating TIME to Sell, Lead, or Manage"

Paper Trails is in plain simple language that any one can follow. It provides an easy to follow step by step process on why you should make electronic records the master. I like the examples, the comparison of the dirt road crossings and the information highway. By the time I finished reading Paper Trails I was excited about electronic records, ERMS, and ECM. Why? Because now I have a clearer understanding of what they are how they work.

Pat Badry, Records Manager

I am currently working with an organization that requires long term retention of their records and that is creating retention schedules that state exactly that. electronic information should be deemed the master and paper should be considered transitory. The statement that rang so true for me was that "employees must be trained to be accountable for their records". In government today not everyone truly believes that statement.

Kerri Bazinet, Records Manager

Concise, highly readable and immediately relevant are my top of mind reactions to Beelby and Roy's offering to the information overloaded, time starved records and information management professional. The business case for the wholesale adoption of electronic records management is expertly outlined and has the force of tried and true records management practice. A must-have title for all Canadian businesses seeking the efficiencies of electronic records management and streamlined corporate compliance.

Margaret Shane, BA, MLIS, Librarian

"*Paper Trails* provides an excellent summary of the benefits of an electronic system for information management within a company."

Harold Taylor, author of "Making Time Work For You."

"I can't imagine a more thorough and valuable book on the subject of Electronic Records. Pat Beelby and Marcel Roy are experts on this material and you will be too when you read their book. This book is truly the standard on Electronic Records!"

Ed Peters, President, 4Profit Institute

Disclaimer

This book is designed to provide information about the subject matter covered. It is sold with the understanding that the publisher and authors are not engaged in rendering legal, accounting or other professional services. If legal or other expert assistance is required, the services of a competent professional should be sought. It is not the purpose of this book to reprint all the information that is otherwise available to authors and other creative people but to complement, amplify and supplement other texts.

Every effort has been made to make this book as complete and as accurate as possible. However, there may be typographical and content mistakes. Therefore, this text should be used only as a general guide and not as the ultimate source on records management and documentary evidence.

Furthermore, this book contains information on records management, electronic document management and documentary evidence only up to the printing date. The purpose of this book is to educate and entertain. The authors and Park Publishing shall have neither liability nor responsibility to any person or entity with respect to any loss or damage caused or alleged to be caused directly or indirectly by the information contained in this book. If you do not wish to be bound by the above, you may return this book to the publisher for a full refund.

We thank Dixie Anderson for her research, editing, writing skills and for giving generously of her time which added so much to this book and our practice in this field.

We want to thank Kim Duke for inspiring us to just get it done, all those who read our consultation draft and gave us feedback, Marietta Miller of www.execugraphx.com for the cover design and Whitney Exton and Carol Fox for the final editing, proofing, and printing setup.

Finally, we want to thank our staff who work so hard in this business with us: Ray Lemont, Lorraine Gorman and Carol Fox.

Table of Contents

About the Authors

We, Marcel Roy and Pat Beelby of TRAC Records Inc., earn our living working with organizations to improve how they manage their information.

We come to this work from very different backgrounds. Marcel Roy has worked his entire career in records management. As technology such as imaging systems emerged to manage information, Marcel recognized that this is the future and he followed the development of what is now called enterprise content management (ECM). Marcel was Director of Records Management for the Province of Alberta, Canada before he started TRAC Records Inc. over 15 years ago. Since then he has consulted in many industries and levels of government and along the way obtained a certificate in information management from the University of Alberta.

While Marcel comes from the records management world, Pat comes from a career in public management where she experienced the frustration of not finding corporate information fast enough, or not at all. Pat spent over twenty years working in government in various management positions, and along the way, she obtained a Masters in public management from the Faculty of Business at the University of Alberta. Her last public management job was with the City of Edmonton, Alberta, Canada. Her responsibilities included overseeing the records management program including managing the city council's records and implementing a then-emerging technology — an electronic document management system. It was here that she and Marcel, hired as a consultant, first met and worked together.

In 1996, Pat changed careers and went into selling electronic document management systems for a business equipment company. During this time, Pat became a Certified Document Management Architech™ (see www.comptia.org). This certification is the first global standard for professional-ism in the imaging and document management industry.

We have worked together in TRAC Records Inc. since 1999. It has been an exciting time for us to collaborate in a field in which we have different points of view and experience. We feel the ER- TRAC Framework that we have developed could not have been developed by just one of us; it is truly a result of a meeting of minds. When asked who the main brain in the company is, our answer is we are equal but different. Frequently, there are opposing opinions, which have resulted in a positive synergy that has led to the best possible solution.

How to Contact the Authors

We are located in Sherwood Park, Alberta, Canada, next door to the city of Edmonton. We would be pleased to answer any questions or receive your comments on the book. We are also available to work with organizations on implementing any part of the ER- TRAC framework and to speak at conferences.

TRAC Records Inc.
#212, 10 Chippewa Road
Sherwood Park, AB T8A 3Y1
780-449-4240

www.tracrecords.ca
www.patbeelby.com
trac@tracrecords.ca

To sign up for our free newsletter, *KeepTRAC*, visit our website www.tracrecords.ca

Foreword

This is a little book, but do not be fooled. It presents an ambitious vision for managing an organization's information to provide a big return on investment. It is a call to action to put paper in its place as a reading medium, not as a storage medium. Let the electronic record be the master record. To do so is to enjoy some powerful benefits for your organization.

The place to start with any major policy, technology and process change is with the business case. We hope this book will inspire you to move ahead with implementing the ER-TRAC™ Framework for information management in your organization.

We want to know what people think of our work and their experience with it, so please do not hesitate to contact us at trac@tracrecords.ca. Also, do not be shy about asking us to work with your organization to implement the ER-TRAC Framework.

Chapter One

Take the ER-TRAC to the Information Highway

"When walking, just walk. When sitting, just sit
Above all, do not wobble." –Ummon, Zen Master

"When managing information electronically, manage it
electronically. When managing information with paper,
manage it with paper. Above all, do not waffle."
–Marcel and Pat

Organizations all over the world are waffling on how they
manage their information. "Not so," you say, "why, just this
year we spent one million dollars on a new electronic *<fill in
the blank>* system. That's not waffling."

That is spending money on one aspect of information
management; what about the documents that support your
state-of-the-art system? Mostly they are paper, right? You

have managed to implement twenty miles of highway and then without warning, with much of your journey ahead, you hit a dirt road. And what happens when you hit dirt roads at highway speeds? You've got it. You go skidding out of control.

We see so many organizations that continue to upgrade their information management systems and never step back to look at the whole picture of information management. The leaders do not seem to ask themselves, "Do we have the information that we really need, can we access it, and do we know where it is?"

Electronic information management systems in organizations are often high-speed highways built at the expense of leaving dirt roads throughout the organization. Those dirt roads are the paper trails. These trails are often inadequate because they are poorly maintained. These information management systems are critically important to businesses but alone they don't serve all the information needs of the organization. When faced with having to present the documentary evidence of their business, organizations frequently fall short of finding what they need and are forced to use the maze of dirt roads. It is time consuming and there are many dead ends. Organizations need to commit to managing all information electronically.

Employees are trained to use the high-speed highways, but they are left to build their own dirt roads to meet much of their information needs. They are not given the policy and technology tools to do otherwise. There has been no peace of mind within these organizations despite spending millions on information management systems because these systems do not give employees all the information they need when and where they need it.

Most organizations have trouble finding information. It takes too long to find it. It is not handy and not where they want it. When employees try to share information, they fight. John never brings back the files on time. Jack never signs out the files. Mary is tired of nagging Jack and John. If they do not care, why should she?

Trouble finding information becomes much bigger than this. It is losing customers because a customer service agent does not have access to the paper file or still on the phone while the customer is in front of him/her. It is not finding all the documents you need to defend your organization in litigation. It is about failing compliance audits because you cannot produce all the documents.

Peace of mind will come when their information highway system spreads out logically from the hub (heart) of the organization. The hub of the organization will direct what information is to be collected and where it goes. Employees will know the entire information highway system and their role in building and maintaining it. There will be access roads to the entire information highway system from afar. The organization will get to its goals entirely on paved roads.

ER-TRAC Framework

The first time we went to write this book we struggled with the need to label what we were recommending because it takes policy, processes, procedures, training and technology together to implement our vision. So we have developed a framework to help you see what we will be talking about in this book. The ER-TRAC Framework pulls together all the elements required to yield the benefits that are included in the chart below. ER-TRAC is a theoretical framework, not a product that you would purchase. It simply shows the elements of our solution that will lead to the specific benefits.

ER-TRAC™ Framework		
Fast TRAC to the high performance workplace		
Policy	**Tools**	
• Employee Accountability	• Enterprise Content Management Software	• Records Creation Matrix
• Electronic Record Master and Paper Transitory	• Corporate Taxonomy	• Information Security Matrix
• Policy and Procedures for Electronic Records as Documentary Evidence	• Retention and Disposition Schedule	• Change Management Plan
Benefits		
• Corporate Peace of Mind	• Compliance Assurance	
• Improved Customer Service	• Increased Security	
• Efficient Processes	• Business Resumption	

What makes the ER-TRAC Framework unique is that we declare paper as transitory and make the electronic record the master record. It takes a combination of policy and tools, which include technology and sound records management and changing management practices, to manage all information electronically. The purpose of the policy is to lay the foundation on which to build the environment necessary to realize the benefits outlined in the last box. When implemented as a total solution using the ER-TRAC Process, the ER-TRAC Framework ensures that the organization receives the benefits we will be talking about in this book (the ER-TRAC Process is outlined in Appendix A).

Paper is Optional

This book calls for a decision to manage all information electronically. Moving to the ER- (Electronic Records) TRAC Framework breaks the cycle of dependency on paper, moving to a less stressful, more intuitive system for managing information. In this framework, paper is optional. It is a transitory medium for reading and carrying about information. The storage and management of all information is in the digital medium. The business processes are digitally automated to gain even more efficiency.

This of course raises all kinds of questions. Is it legal? Your lawyers have always said you must keep documents. What happens 25 years from now if you documents are electronic? You worry about accessing the information in the future. You think that it will be years before you can afford the technology. This book will demonstrate that you can afford to move to total electronic information management and that your worries can be addressed.

The ER-TRAC Framework is about much more than making paper optional. It is about:

- access to your organization's information from near and far;
- securing information from improper access;
- planning for disasters and having the information you need for business resumption;
- quick retrieval of all the information that your organization holds;
- not having to search high and low for files;
- not hunting through someone's computer directory for a critical document on a day he/she is away;
- providing immediate and excellent personalized service to your customers;
- being confident that you can comply with all legal and regulatory requirements; and
- having a cost-effective information management system that will increase your productivity.

Ten Reasons not to Use Paper

1. The time it takes a person to put paper in a paper folder, walk over to a filing cabinet, and put it into the drawer.
2. The time it takes others to go to the filing cabinet, take it out (if they can find it) and walk back to their offices.
3. Filing cabinets and filing shelves take up a lot office space.
4. You need a photocopy machine to copy paper.
5. You need a facsimile machine to send paper over the telephone lines.

6. You need a scanner if you want to email paper.
7. You can only search for words on the page by reading the document.
8. Paper is not what it used to be. It does not age well.
9. Why would you want to use paper when you have nearly everything you need already to manage information electronically?
10. The truth of the matter is, at least 50% of electronic records and emails have never been printed. You do not have proper records unless the electronic records are managed within an electronic document management system.

Bonus reason: Save the forests.

Three Reasons to Keep Paper Around

1. It is the easiest medium to read.
2. It is convenient to carry some information around on paper.
3. When working on a project, it is convenient to have paper spread around you.

The ER-TRAC Framework is based on years of experience with organizations that have professionally managed networks in place. We would expect that the information technology of an organization might include back up systems, database applications such as financial systems, human resources management applications, customer relationship management (CRM) solutions and customized applications for the operation of the organization. All of these, and others not mentioned, must meet the requirements for documentary evidence so that the electronic record can be accepted as the master record for the information it contains.[1] The information in these systems is referred to as "structured".

All supporting documents, and in fact all corporate documents should be managed digitally and be acceptable as documentary evidence. These documents are referred to as "unstructured" information.

The goal of this book is to hopefully motivate managers in organizations to adopt the ER-TRAC Framework for information management. At the very least, we want organizations to realize that information management is records management, and that an information/records management policy framework has to be put in place.

Does your organization have a policy which clearly states that records/information is an asset of your organization and that every employee has accountability for managing that asset?

Records management is not sexy and information technology is. Records management is all too often left to the administrative assistants, while information management is handled by information technologists. Today, in order to meet compliance requirements, all managers and CEOs must become sophisticated information managers with an understanding of records management principles and practices. Increasingly legislation, such as Sarbanes - Oxley, are forcing organizations to improve records management.

---

[1] The requirements for records as documentary evidence will be discussed again in Chapter Six.

Many, if not most, people working in organizations think that their documents are not records until they "publish" them. They think that they can have personal information at work. This is not a position that the courts will likely view in the same way. Treat every scrap of information, whether it is digital, on paper, on audio tape, on microfilm, or carved in stone, as a record of the organization. Do not record anything which is not professional in tone and content.

You will want to implement our framework for the business value you will get from it. You will see improved customer service and remarkable savings throughout your business. Consider that all employees use information. All you have to do is incrementally improve the efficiency with which they get that information and you can have big savings in staff time, paper, duplicating and storage costs. Add to that all the benefits you will read about in this book and you are going to have a nimble, lean organization that will forge ahead of the competition.

If we have not convinced you yet about managing information electronically read the next chapters. We will talk about the business benefits that result from our frame-work and how to upgrade your dirt roads to the paved roads of the information highway.

ER-TRAC Tips

- Electronic information management cannot be confined to one department or one set of documents. It is an integrated process that must consider all corporate documents whether paper or electronic.
- Employee accountability, corporate policies and procedures, a master electronic record, and meeting the requirements for documentary evidence create a foundation for implementing efficient and effective information management solutions.

- Implemented using the appropriate tools, the ER-TRAC Framework will provide real, measurable benefits.

Chapter Two

Fast TRAC your Customers

To succeed in competitive markets, organizations have to focus on the customer. Better service is about more personalized service and immediate gratification. Customers are becoming more sophisticated and more demanding and if you let them get away, your competition will take care of them.

Universal Access to Documents from Any Location

With the ER-TRAC Framework in place, all customer agents will have any information within the organization that is required to deal with the customer in front of them available through their computers. That could be information in the customer relationship management database or the last letter they wrote to the CEO or the form they filled out on the Internet.

Access to Information = Faster Service

The ER-TRAC Framework ensures that all policies and procedures will be online and fully searchable. The policies and procedures will be up-to-date, as one person will be responsible for keeping this version current at all times. There will be accountability for keeping these documents current. Gone will be the out-of-date binders of policies and procedures, the updates that always fall out of the binder when it is picked up. If your organization has progressed beyond the papers binder to policies and procedures on an intranet, how up-to-date and how searchable is it? Does the person who is responsible for maintaining these documents have to rely on someone with technical expertise to upload them? Does the organization have a printed copy of the document which indicates when these became effective and when they were revised? Unless you follow the guidelines for documentary evidence, your electronic document may not be accepted as evidence.

Access to In-Process Documents

These same customer agents can determine if the customer's request has been processed by checking into the automated business process software to find out how far the request has gone and where it may have stopped.

Less Time Looking for Information = More Time with Customers

When customer agents can access the information they need quickly, they have more time to spend with each customer and to sell more products or services. They can also serve more customers in a day. When customer agents can look at all the information and follow what the customer is talking about, the organization gains credibility.

Access Customer Documents from any Location

We have credit union clients in rural locations in Saskatchewan, Canada. These credit unions have members who are highly mobile and need to travel to different towns for their shopping, health and business needs. They do not want to be tied to their home branch. This can be resolved by providing access of all records from anywhere via a web browser.

For example, if a client is buying a piece of machinery in one town, he can go the credit union in that town to obtain his loan. The loan officer may be able to find some information on current loans in the banking system, but will also need to see the member's file for specific information on security for the current loan and other documented arrangements made at the time of the loan. When using the ER-TRAC Framework and the documents online, the loan officer can access everything he/she needs, instead of having to request the information and wait one to two days for it to arrive by courier. All of the new information will be captured into the system and will be immediately accessible to authorized personnel at all other branches. Authorized access is set out in the security matrix.

The loan officer is able to finalize the loan with the customer in front of him/her. He/she uses automated business process software to create the loan documents.

All of the member's basic information is automatically filled into the forms and the member signs digitally. The document is created and saved into the electronic records management system (ERMS).[2] This is a legal master electronic document that can be emailed to the member or the member can go home with a printed copy.

Many organizations find themselves in a position of having to give copies of documents to customers who have misplaced or lost them. In the example of credit unions, customers may lose their copy of a tax document. It takes time to retrieve a document from a paper file, copy it, replace it in the file, and put it back on the shelf. Instead, the customer service agent can simply call it up on the ERMS, print it out and quickly move on to the next customer.

Can you imagine how much more satisfied this credit union's customers are with the new system, and with getting fast and reliable service from knowledgeable staff? Would you like this for your customers?

Ensure Long-Term Access

In government, there is the challenge of retrieving documents for access to information requests. We have worked with child welfare records where requests for information may come thirty years after the child was in custody of the government. The ER-TRAC Framework ensures long-term access and accountability for maintaining proper records.

---

[2]Throughout this book we use ERMS to refer to electronic document management systems and/or electronic records management systems which are types of enterprise content management (ECM) software.

Customers have Direct Access to their Documents

A big advantage of having all documents within an ERMS with a web interface is that clients can be given access to organization documents or to documents that you are holding for them. In the case of steel manufacturing, the manufacturer has to pass along extensive documentation including drawings and mill test reports. If the client is given access to the system, he/she can download the documents into his/her own system and it saves everyone time. For example, we know of a large petrochemical company that requires its suppliers, including consultants, to store all of their project-related documents in the company's electronic records management system to make the documents readily available to anyone who needs them.

Real-Time Interactivity with Customers

Government agencies can give customers access to interactive systems for paying bills, applying for licenses, registering for programs and even for booking facilities. Think of the staff time that is saved and think of the convenience for the client who does not have to line up and can interact with the system any time of the day or night. If you provide this access now, are you sure that the electronic records created meet legal requirements?

The ER-TRAC Framework ensures that clients get fast, professional, reliable and consistent customer service from any location, even their own office or home. When the quality and efficiency of service improves, your profits will increase. But ER-TRAC Framework also provides great benefits within your organization.

ER-TRAC Tips

- Improved customer service means greater profits.
- The ER-TRAC Framework yields faster service, access from any location, more knowledgeable front-line staff, long-term and remote access, direct access by customers, real-time interactivity and consistency in service.

Chapter Three

TRAC Business Processes and Improve Productivity

Ron is a project manager and his project is running behind schedule. He needs to have all the drawings for the construction of an office building ready for a deadline. His project is but one of many large projects in the company. Ron is located in an area of economic boom and everyone in his company is going nuts with the business.

Ron needs more computer-assisted drawings (CAD) operators to produce his drawings. He has managed to find two suitable candidates who will start in two weeks. They need many things in place for them when they start including a phone line, a network ID, a computer, office space, a parking space, a security ID, an email address, and enrolment in the benefits plan. Normally this would take lots of Ron's time — getting in touch with everyone responsible through email or phone and trying to remember to get back in touch to make sure things are completed.

Create Efficiencies in Workflow

Instead, Ron opens the new employee workflow application on his computer, enters the information once and hits the go button. At any time, Ron can see how things are progressing but otherwise he has no further concerns unless contacted. In a few minutes from when he opened the application, he is back on the job. How easy is that? Moreover, consider how much his organization has saved by freeing his time to work on what he does best. There is the tangible benefit of less billable time from administration to the project, but what about the intangible benefit of sparing him hours of bureaucratic frustrations? It is priceless.

The form he filled in was electronic and it just flowed through the system branching out to all the people who needed to be involved. No one in the organization had to re-enter the employee information Ron provided. It was electronically forwarded to the appropriate information systems and to the appropriate people.

Get Rid of Stacks of Forms

By using ER-TRAC Framework, you will not have paper forms in your organization. You will not have space taken up with stacks of forms. You will not have to destroy those stacks of paper because of fees, a change in name, program or any other kind of change.

Enter Information Once

You may have a number of your forms online for employees to access now. Are they re-entering information that is already in a system within your organization? Are they printing it off to fax it somewhere — or worse, walking with it somewhere? There are electronic forms with different capabilities. Some are just an electronic copy that you can print to fill out with pen. Others allow you to type the information onto a form, but that information is not transferable. In the ER-TRAC Framework, the electronic forms are part of an automated business process software solution and the software will talk to other databases within the organization's information technology environment. Therefore, information can be transferred and entered into another database automatically as needed.

Direct Input from Clients

How is customer information entered into your system? Is one of your staff entering this information into a database? In our framework, the client enters information on the Internet and submits it. If that does not work for your company, make computers at points of service available for your staff to do the same thing. In Canada, the unemployment agency has computers in the waiting areas and clients are expected to enter their basic information into the computer. When the information is submitted, it is immediately validated automatically. Remember, paper slows down the flow of information dramatically.

Within the ER-TRAC Framework there is some basic required software and depending on your business needs, more sophisticated software can be added. For example, there is the universal problem of what to do with email. Email has virtually eliminated letters and memorandums. Therefore, emails are records of business transactions and approvals for action to be taken. Emails can also be the lowest form of communication you ever receive, such as spam. Sophisticated software can auto-classify emails as they come into the organization, deciding where they should be stored within the electronic records management system.

Handle Paper Mail Efficiently

Have you ever thought about the cost in staff time for handling paper mail? Instead of mail being opened, it could be scanned, entered into the ERMS and notification would be sent to you about it. Before you even touch it, it is stored securely. There is no delay, no worry about what you might do with it. You can look at it and forward to it one of your staff to handle. You can set a due date and let the system monitor it for you. You can get on with other more important things to do.

Dump your Facsimile Machine

How do you handle facsimile documents? How costly is it to have the facsimile machine watched? How often do the faxes not reach the rightful recipient? We have successfully eliminated our facsimile machine. However, many businesses still rely on facsimile machines.. Therefore, we send and receive faxes through an online fax service eliminating the need for a facsimile data line and machine. This online service provides the additional benefit of delivering our faxes to us via email. Even during our speaking engagement in Barcelona, Spain we received faxes via our email. Alternatively, facsimile software can be installed on your network. Encouraging your suppliers to email or fax your invoices is one way to reduce the scanning of paper and easily stored within your ERMS.

Track Correspondence

Correspondence is a universal problem for organizations. Governments have to deal with customers writing to different people in the same organization about the same issue. These people may well work their way down the organization's hierarchy starting with elected officials, senior bureaucrats and all the way to a front line caseworker. It can be embarrassing for the organization when a customer receives conflicting answers. With all correspondence including paper mail and emails being captured within an ERMS system and monitored through the automated business process software, it is possible to search to see if others have received the same or similar correspondence. You can see who is working on responses and what is being drafted. You can also monitor deadlines for responding. If everyone answers consistently, but does so over a period of three or four weeks, it does not create a good impression either.

Find a Document in Process

Just as correspondence is a universal challenge for organizations, so is anything that involves review or approval by several people. Contracts and agreements often waste time when employees hunt for the contract somewhere in the approval process: is it at finance services, administrative services, legal services, purchasing or lost in transit?

When you look in the automated business process system, it will tell you exactly where the contract is. It will notify those required for approval and tell them their deadline. If one of the people required to approve the agreement is away, the notification system is designed to automatically re-route the document. You are also not wasting time contacting staff just to find out if they have seen something or not.

Transparency of Processes

Transparency of processes is a commonly heard term. It means that the processes of an organization must be easy to access and easy to see. The more the processes are automated, the more assured the custodians of the organization can be that the corporate rights are protected. In proving compliancy, it is a big asset to be able to show how processes are managed. Automated processes and the resulting efficient handling of records also mean this proof is found easily and quickly. This saves time and results in increased productivity.

Automating processes is about saving time moving information around and putting it places, such as other databases. It is not about stopping employees from moving about or even talking to each other. It is about taking away paper shuffling and leaving time for more meaningful, productive exchanges.

Faster, More Complete Retrieval

Time is wasted looking for information. What does that really mean? A manager asks an administrative assistant, who started six months ago, for a report written eighteen months ago. He/she has no idea where it was filed. When the best guesses do not yield it, a call goes out to other office staff who drop what they are doing and look for their copy. How much better would it be if the manager could have typed key words into a search engine accessible right on his desktop computer and have the report appear a few seconds later? The report may represent a fifty thousand dollar investment of the organization, but where is it now?

What about when the pressure is not on? Is retrieving information an issue? Yes, it is. Time is lost every day trying to find files and documents on networks, in desk drawers, cabinets and overflowing in-boxes. Have you ever tried going through someone's directory system when he/she is away from the office to figure out what he/she named a file?

Are you in a business where your customer waits you have to get a file while the customer waits? When customers phone in do your customer service agents have to hang up to get a file from the file room and then try to get the customer back on the phone? Imagine dealing with the customer's request for information or processing an order by calling the file up on the screen. It is a matter of a few clicks of a mouse to send off the order via email.

How does this compare with walking to the file room, interrupted along the way, finding the file, taking it back to the desk and starting the game of telephone tag with the customer? If the agent doesn't get hold of the customer and lets the file sit on the desk, what happens when the customer calls back and gets a different agent and that agent goes to the file room to look for the file and it is not there?

Knowledge workers work with information as bricklayers work with brick and mortar. Can you imagine how long it would take to build a brick wall if the tradesman had to retrieve specific bricks one at a time?

Standard Taxonomy and Intuitive Retrieval

What are the factors that make retrieving information so difficult? The quantity of information and how we choose to group records (classify or index) are the main challenges. What makes perfect sense for one staff member may not for another, then the challenge of finding records years later. Are grocery stores arranged alphabetically? Where do you find toothpicks in different store chains? Don't you appreciate it when stores of the same chain are organized consistently? In the ER-TRAC Framework, information is organized in a standard taxonomy that is applied throughout the whole organization regardless of location or format of records.

There is also the challenge of physical location. You may know where a file should be but what if it is not there? Often files are lost by simply misfiling while others go on sleepovers. Using an electronic records management system allows you to search either by subject (corporate taxonomy) or by key words in the document making searching more intuitive and easier to locate.

Always Work on the Right Version

Version control is a big problem for many organizations. We have seen the most costly evidence of this in companies who have blueprints. If an engineer designs a system or a part for a manufacturing or refinery operation from the wrong version of a blueprint, the costs can be enormous. A refinery can be shut down for a new part to be installed only to have it not fit because it was designed from the wrong version of the blueprint. How can this happen? It happens when renovations are made and the old as-built plans have been left in place as current. You will not want to destroy the as-built plans, but you will want them labelled as such and stored.

Blueprints are created now through computer applications. There can be confusion over versions as blueprints are created and revised. One CAD technician told us about working on the wrong version of a drawing, so the day of work was a complete waste. How costly is that to the company, not to mention how demoralizing for the employee?

Versions are not restricted to drawings. Every electronic document can be saved as a version, and frequently is. Most people do that by simply renaming the file. When they think it is final, they rename it. But what if it is not final and their boss changes it and saves it to his/her directory as something else? In an ERMS (electronic records management system), versions can be saved under the same name and number with various authors and notes attached. When the document is finalized, it is simply a matter of deleting all earlier versions. This greatly reduces clutter on the network and chances of embarrassment or financial loss due to working from the wrong version.

Foster Better Decision-Making

What is better than having all of the information required to make a decision at your fingertips? Records, policies, procedures, financial information, history and previous studies are available to make an informed decision.

Facilitate Distribution of Information

Distributing information within and outside the organization is key to competing in today's markets. The sum total effect of the ER-TRAC Framework is to make all required information quickly and easily accessible to those who need it and have a right to it, wherever they are.

ER-TRAC Tips

- More efficient internal business processes and improvements in workflow mean increased profits.
- The ER-TRAC Framework allows you to enter information once, have direct input by clients, track work in process, track correspondence, get rid of stacks of paper, and always use the right version.
- Standard taxonomy allows faster retrieval that is more intuitive.
- Using the ER-TRAC Framework facilitates the distribution of information and fosters more informed decision-making.

Chapter Four

Keep on TRAC with the Law

How does an organization prove that it did something? It has to provide documentary proof. That is the bottom line yet organizations do not consider managing documents a top priority. Paper trails, that were once the information roadways, are not what they used to be. Now that electronic information has emerged, money has been diverted from paper document management to electronic document management and managers have lost sight of creating a documentary trail. This happened unintentionally when the allure of technology swept people away, but the result was that records management principles were lost. At the same time, competitive forces were causing organizations to downsize and many of the positions responsible for managing paper records were eliminated. The result has been that organizations are always struggling to find records whenever legal action is threatened or to meet compliance obligations.

Organizations must have a Legal Record of their Activities

What if the organization cannot find the documents that prove they have complied legally, or what if these documents were destroyed? What are the consequences if not all of the documents can be found? This might not sound like a big deal, but what if your organization is a social services agency that is being sued because a child has died due to negligence in a foster home? What is the legal liability if you are not able to provide all the documentation supporting the decision to place that child? What if you are missing a few documents that provided testimonials regarding the adequacy of care?

Find Documents Now and in the Future

Increasingly, laws are being passed which have requirements for the management of records. There is now environmental protection legislation that requires some records to be saved for twenty-five years and permanently in some cases. Most organizations are aware of the need to keep records for financial reasons but forget that there may be other laws that require them to keep records for shorter or longer periods.

Policy Direction to Employees for Record Accountability

Knowing you have to save records is one thing, but doing so successfully is quite another matter. Our framework builds in employee accountability to create and manage the records, because organizations frequently do not actually tell their employees that they have to document their business transactions. We have read risk management articles that emphasize what should not be created, but do not say what records must be created. It is not just a matter of deciding what to create but also deciding how long to keep records and what information has enduring value. In all instances, records must not be destroyed or transferred without proper authorization.

These guidelines must be communicated to employees. The ER-TRAC Framework ensures that corporate policies clearly provide direction to employees to create records of their business transactions. It is important to be perfectly clear about what records are to be created and how long they are to be kept.

It is ironic that when organizations respond to a regulatory requirement for managing their records, it is the resulting improved records management practices and the consequent improved productivity that most impresses them. A senior official, in the Canadian government, told us that civil servants thought the sky was falling in when the freedom of information legislation was introduced. Now the same civil servants are saying that it had not been a big deal and the new practices allow them to more readily find records.

Authorized Access to Protect Privacy

Governments for some time have had to deal with freedom of information and protection of privacy legislation. Recently the private sector has had to deal with protection of their customers' information. The challenge of this legislation is identifying what information the organization has and keeping it secure. How can an organization find all of its information when much of it is on individual computers and in office filing cabinets? Any search for information in that situation is time consuming and therefore costly. With the implementation of our framework, the information will be there, easily searchable for anyone authorized to access it. It will also be possible to protect the information by setting security on it. The audit trail that is kept within the document management system or database application will show exactly who has accessed it and what was done.

When employees have easy access to up-to-date policies and procedures, they can more easily comply with requirements. Their work can be easily monitored through searches by supervisors.

Find all the Relevant Records and all Related Records

When the court cases start, so does the search for records. Liability can be greatly reduced by finding all the related records. Costs can be reduced, too, by finding those records quickly. The records tell a story. What happens if that story is not told completely? For example, an engineer writes a memo saying a building is not safe. Then there are subsequent problems in the building, and the owner is sued. The owner made changes that made it safe and the engineer subsequently wrote another memo saying his concerns were addressed. Now the owner can only find the first memo and not the second one. The owner is in a very risky position.

If in the discovery process of the litigation, an organization is ordered to release all of its records on the case, failure to do so can affect the outcome of the case and the credibility of the organization. Look at these quotes from the FBI Press

Room regarding the Timothy McVeigh investigation, after the FBI was accused of failing to provide all the documentation it had.[3]

> "The FBI committed a serious error by not ensuring that every piece of information was properly accounted for and, when appropriate, provided to the prosecutors so they could fulfill their discovery obligations."

> "We simply cannot allow the dazzle of technology and the complexity and breadth of our mission to dim the focus on a function that goes to the very core of what we do. In short, this episode demonstrated that the mundane must be done as well as the spectacular."

Retrieve and Destroy all Documents According to Retention Schedules

The ER-TRAC Framework deals with when to dispose of records according to records management retention schedules. It is in the best interests of organizations to keep records for as long as they need to and then destroy them. The length of retention will be governed by legislation and by business requirements. Just as you will want to retrieve all the records when you need to, you will want to retrieve all records for destruction at the appropriate time. Managing information within an ERMS, you will be able to do a search

---

[3] Statement for the Record of Louis J. Freeh, former Director, Federal Bureau of Investigation on FBI File Management before the House Appropriations Subcommittee, Washington, D.C. Congressional Statement. 2001 FBI File Management, May 16, 2001.

of all repositories of information for specific words and the linked documents. For example, you can pull up all documents on a project that are slated for destruction.

In preparing for litigation, you can search for all related documents for release. Increasingly litigators are getting the permission of the courts to search certain drives on the networks of organizations or files of certain custodians of information to find information that may not have been released to them. You want to make sure that you have it first.

If there is information beyond its retention, not appropriately created or simply lost, you will lose credibility and worse, lose the case. Your organization could lose hundreds of thousands or even millions of dollars.

Know who Authorizes Destruction of Documents

Remember recent headlines where managers were accused of ordering destruction of paper documents? In our framework, destruction of that nature would not be possible. Security to protect the destruction of documents would be in place, and all that could happen is that information would be electronically queued for destruction. A trusted administrator would be the one who would do the actual destruction. According to best records management practices, there would be a record of the information that is destroyed and who approved its destruction. Our framework protects the overall interests of the corporate body.

In this case directing the destruction of the information is not just a case of bad judgement, it is contrary to the law which requires the opposite action. That is, the law requires a litigation hold be placed on the destruction of records when you first know, or ought to have known, about pending litigation. That does not mean when you are served with the papers, it means when you know a claim is likely. That could be when an initial demand is received or a notice letter, or something of that nature.

The litigation hold extends to electronic records management systems where you need to have the functionality to change the destruction date or otherwise ensure that the records do not get destroyed. What happens if you go ahead and destroy the records? The law calls it "spoliation of evidence". In simple terms it means that the worst will be assumed. Let's say it was being disputed whether the proper grade of materials was used and all the invoices were destroyed relating to the purchase of the materials. The law would assume that those invoices would prove that substandard materials were purchased.

We interviewed a small business owner who was suing a large organization over a patent infringement. He had received a number of boxes of information from the organization. He sat in his basement night after night, scanning the documents and converting them into text files. Then he searched under keywords. He organized them and turned the information over to his lawyers. When the trial began, the organization — which obviously had not really looked at what they had passed to him — had staff testifying that certain records were not available in the company. The lawyers for the small business owner produced the documents. This happened over and over again until the judge intervened and requested that the small business owner give the organization their documents back so the trial could move on.

The difference was that the files were now organized, inventoried and searchable. If the organization had a proper records management program they would have known what they had given him. If they had gone a step further with an ERMS they could have gathered the records swiftly and copied them electronically rather than handling the paper. The owner won the case and was awarded millions of dollars. Subsequently, I am told it was overturned in appeal, but can you imagine the work that had to been done at the large organization to overcome the file fiasco and to regain their footing in the legal action. The organization also had the added expense of the legal fees of a second trial.

Let's look in detail at what would happen if you were a manager in an organization that was being sued because a structure it built collapsed. Similar questions and problems could arise with any product or service in your organization. In litigation, through the discovery phase, you might be requested to release all of the information related to the building of the structure. Would you and your staff be able to find it *all*?

First, you would think of project management files. The project was completed five years ago. Where are the files now? If you contracted out the project management function, were you careful in getting all copies of the files? Is that company still in business?

Don't forget too, as mentioned earlier in the chapter, that you must immediately put a litigation hold on all information related to the project as soon as you are aware of the possibility of litigation.

If you find the project files, can you trust that all the records are there? Are there records in accounts payable that would cover the purchase of the materials? What staff members were involved? Does the human resources department have their employee files? Were they trained in manufacturer's requirements? When and by whom? Did they attend the training? What was in the curriculum of the course? Where are the contracts? Does legal have them? Where are the final drawings? You may have given printed plans to the customer, but did your staff also print copies for filing? Are the drawings still on the network and could you prove that they have not been altered? What about the purchasing specifications? Could you prove that the right materials were specified? You might need to verify exactly what the purchasing department released to bidders. You might need to show any variations in what was received in your building materials.

This is happening more and more in a world demanding compliance to legal regulation. This extends to privacy legislation and any quality control standard, such as International Organization for Standardization (ISO). The point is this — you would need to look for information in every corner of organization, literally and figuratively. You ask others in your organization to look for information, but will they? They might be very busy or not too concerned with your problems. If the paper files are found, what kind of effort is going to be required to photocopy, reassemble, organize and inventory them? What about the search of the network for related emails and business application documents?

Establish Consistent Direction and Policy

We have a "Life is not Fair" rule of electronic records. It goes like this: any document on your network *may* be acceptable as documentary evidence, but if you want to increase the probability of acceptance then you must follow the guidelines for electronic records as documentary evidence. This means that you <u>cannot</u> afford do nothing. You may think you have dealt with your electronic records but if you are not lucky, they will be used against you one way or another.

This requires a commitment to policies, procedures and processes as well as an investment in technology to meet these guidelines. If you choose not to manage electronic records as documentary evidence and rely on paper originals, it does not preclude your network documents from having to be disclosed in a discovery process. It also means that if you want your electronic documents to stand as evidence they might not be accepted. Yet the other side's lawyer can ask for these records.

Communicate Policies throughout your Organization

Within the justice and regulatory worlds, there is recognition for an organization setting a direction in policy, developing associated procedures and processes and then ensuring compliance through periodic follow-up. There is legal credibility in being able to show that whatever an employee may have done is consistent with the policies and procedures of the organization.

Protect yourself by Automating Processes

Within the regulatory environment, there is increasingly more emphasis and consistency in the processes. The ISO standards, when recently revised, placed more emphasis on process. By automating processes through automated business process software, your organization can go a long way to protecting itself legally.

ER-TRAC Tips

The ER-TRAC Framework ensures documents are accepted as documentary evidence by:

1. Ensuring regulatory compliance by:

- archival and oversight activities;
- create an audit trail;
- establish a record of community expectations of acceptable behaviour;
- derive policy from business activities;
- comply with privacy legislation; and
- ensure documents adhere to policies, procedures and industry standards.

2. Protecting an organization during litigation by:

- access to precedents cases;
- facilitate discovery process;
- reduce liability if all relevant information found;
- identify and retrieve legal opinions;
- protect legal interests by placing holds on destruction of records related to a subject matter immediately upon becoming aware of the possibility of litigation in that matter; and
- protect copyright by storing copies offsite.

Chapter Five

TRAC Security and Storage

Harold hung up the phone. He could not believe what he had just heard. It was the middle of the night but he called his partner Lloyd immediately, "Lloyd, the office is on fire. No, I am not kidding. The police just called. I will meet you down there."

The fire destroyed the three-storey office building where their business was. The partners were well-insured so insurance replaced their furniture, equipment and computers. However, the fire had destroyed all their client files. Three months later, they were still not drawing any salary from their business as they struggled to rebuild from a cold start.

Would your Business Survive a Disaster?

If your organization has been following routine network practices, the information on your servers will have been backed up and stored somewhere offsite. But it is surprising how many companies do not have an offsite copy. Some businesses have come through a disaster with not even a client list intact.

But what of the paper files? They are gone. These are often the most valuable information assets. They could include clients' files with all of the contracts, plans, correspondence and case histories; or project files with specifications, drawings, change orders and all relevant information on the project; or the vital records and history of your organization including board of directors' minutes, bylaws and in organization documents.

Microfilm, Photocopy, Scan — the Same Process

The point is that your paper could be gone tomorrow. Does that mean you should copy all your paper files? It would be expensive. You may ask, why not microfilm the documents? Microfilm has been a great way to store documents for long periods. There are advocates who say it is still the best way to store information for fifty to one hundred years.

Consider this, though. Microfilming, photocopying and scanning are the same processes. The only difference is the output: microfilm, microfiche, paper or a scanned image. Microfilm requires special equipment to view and print. It does not give you the immediate access at every customer agent's desk. However, every office worker now has a computer and access to scanned images can be very fast.

Converting paper files to scanned images is certainly part of the ER-TRAC Framework. However, we do not advocate scanning all paper. There are significant costs to converting paper and they can be higher than the implementation of our framework. We recommend to clients to scan on a day forward basis, except for paper files that are retrieved frequently and for records that are required for business continuation and are of enduring value. The paper documents that are not retrieved or retrieved infrequently should be held to live out their retention as paper. If they are taking up too much room then they can go to a records centre until it is time for their disposal.

Paper Takes up Space

How much space do paper files take up? A four-drawer file cabinet takes up five square feet of office space and holds the equivalent of one CD of information.

Paper Costs Ten Times More

In addition to the cost of space for managing paper, you have to take into consideration the retrieval costs, supplies, and maintenance costs. We have conducted cost benefit analyses that demonstrate that the cost of managing paper records is ten times the cost of managing electronic records.

We have a credit union client with fifteen branches who scanned all paper, and now captures all electronic documents into the ERMS system. The documents use 75 gigabytes of storage space. Now, this storage is not as cheap as the 120 gigabyte drive you might have bought for your home computer, as it is stored on a server on a much more expensive drive, but it is still very affordable.

Converting Records Space to Office Space

Why do we care about getting of rid of filing cabinets? They take up a lot of floor space overall in an organization. Think of the cost savings when workspaces are created after the cabinets are taken away. If a move to acquire more space can be avoided, the savings mount up. Sellers of paper filing solutions will give you suggestions about more space-efficient systems. In one instance, we compared the cost of rolling shelving and found that we could implement an electronic records management solution for the cost of the shelving. There are even more savings that can accrue when staff are able to stay put and retrieve the documents from their desktop computers.

Know what to Save and what to Destroy

Business application documents use server space. Emails are one of the biggest space hogs. The challenge with emails is that many are just junk mail; however, there are others which are business-critical records of a business transaction or decision. These have to be managed and the others destroyed. To ensure that emails will be considered as documentary evidence, they have to be managed within the kind of electronic environment recommended in the ER-TRAC Framework. Remember the "Life is not Fair" rule of electronic records discussed earlier (see p. 29). If you do not destroy junk or emails that are not needed they may end up embarrassing you.

Server space is inexpensive compared to paper. So why are we worried about saving space in servers? The problem is that there is so much duplication and very little planned destruction or archiving of documents. So, networks become like a basement with everyone dumping all their stuff into one place. Eventually you cannot find anything except the current documents you are working on.

Authorized Access Only

When we talk to people about our framework, we are
frequently asked about hackers. Certainly, hackers are a
threat to any organization's network. Presumably, there is
security in place to prevent hackers from getting into the
network. The security that is suitable for other applications
currently on the servers will generally be adequate for ECM
software.

People lose track of the amount of information that is within
databases and worry about documents being accessed. The
security used in our framework is at the trusted administrator
level, which is typical in nearly all organizations. However,
the security within your electronic records and business
process systems can be very flexible and set up with very
precise guidelines for access to the information. If someone
tries to find out if information is in the system and he/she
does not have access, he/she will not know it is there. Access
can vary from none to read only to copy to edit. An audit
trail keeps track of the access to the document ensuring that
you can verify who has accessed it and what changes he/she
may have made.

Have you any idea who may have looked at or even
photocopied your paper files? A sales representative who is
moving to another company may secretly copy or print off
customer and other proprietary lists. There is no way you can
prove that it was done short of finding the person with the
papers in his/her possession. Within our framework, either
the sales representative would not have access to the
information or the audit trail with his/her name in it would
show the mass copying, printing or emailing of the
information.

Have you ever wished that you could provide access to some of your electronic documents to specific people and let them copy the information, but not permanently alter the document? That is the purpose of providing different levels of security through an electronic records management system. This level of control cannot be implemented effectively in a manual system.

What about employees who wipe out all of their electronic documents as they leave a job? If all documents have been printed off and filed away, it is not as big a problem, assuming someone knows where to look. However, no one wants to start over inputting form letters and large documents such as reports, union contracts and legal agreements. We have a friend in labour relations who was responsible for the contract with a major union. When she was on holidays, the administrative assistants decided that the contract needed to have its formatting cleaned up. They destroyed the original electronic document and created a new, freshly-typed one. The consequence was that as our friend headed into union negotiations she had no master electronic copy from the last round. She had to spend days proofreading the new document. If there were any errors introduced that she did not catch, the union could have accused her of acting in bad faith by trying to sneak through changes. With the ER-TRAC Framework, documents can be protected from destruction and from editing changes.

Store Back-up Copies Offsite

Another advantage of the ER-TRAC Framework is that all of your records can be backed up readily. There is still a belief in the business world that hard drive space is expensive and that it is cheaper to store paper. It is a myth. What is expensive, anyway? We define expensive as not having a business case to justify the expenditure. We will be talking about the business case more in chapters six and eight. Based on the business case there is nothing expensive about implementing the ER-TRAC Framework. Is paper cheap to manage? It is ten times ,ore expensive to manage than electronically. If you were to add up the floor space used for filing cabinets, the filing supplies and equipment required, you would be amazed at the cost. Moreover, you still have limited access and do not have a duplicate copy of everything.

Once everything is electronic, making copies and storing back-ups anywhere in the world is easy. The possibilities for business continuity in case of disaster are exciting. You can be back in business as soon as you can get equipment. Off-site storage does not have to be expensive or complicated. We know of a physician who uses a USB removable storage device to store her network information every night and takes it home for offsite storage.

Don't Just Treat the Symptoms

We see a lot of money wasted on treating the symptoms of inadequate information management. There is not much money invested in dealing with the proliferation of electronic documents. Electronic documents are generally not managed at all in organizations. Sharing consists of emailing copies of documents. Emails are sent, with documents attached, all over the organization and stored countless times on the network. In our framework, links to the documents are sent and people access only one copy. Users will have a timeframe to put their emails into the repository before they are automatically removed from their inboxes. Employees must be trained to be accountable for their records. It is important to the overall success of the business. Purchasing tools to manage narrow management problems like high volume email repositories, particular document types like engineering drawings and specific email challenges can waste money. There are off-the-shelf electronic records systems that can manage electronic drawings along with all the other information in the organization. We see businesses with dedicated staff who very carefully manage operational records for ISO certification. This is good but it can be costly for so few records and usually ignores all other records. Implementing the ER-TRAC Framework throughout the organization would give a much greater payback on investment.

Digital Preservation and Legacy Planning

There are valid questions raised about long-term access to electronic information. Nearly every organization has a story to tell about losing access to records because of technology change.

The biggest proponents of managing information electronically are governments who have realized the efficiencies in electronic information management with their massive databases. They are doing extensive work in the field of legacy planning. You have only to go to www.archives.gov and search for digital preservation to see the work that has been done in this area. Digital preservation has become a field of specialization and standards are being developed.

Within the ER-TRAC Framework we advocate using industry file formats as much as possible to enable migration and to ensure access to documents, even when the technology changes. We believe it is important to get a handle on your information and treat it like the asset it is. Have an inventory and manage its lifecycle. Have your inventory on a must-keep basis only.

ER-TRAC Call to Action

We are advocating a commitment to the electronic master record because organizations are drifting, in a very inefficient way, towards that anyway. Strictly speaking, if you are not following the guidelines for electronic records as documentary evidence you should be printing all your information like all emails, all word processing, spreadsheets and presentation documents. That is why we say make a decision; manage all your information electronically and put in place all the tools, policies and training required. The result will be a savings in storage costs and an increase in the confidence of the security in the organization's most valuable assets.

ER-TRAC Tips

- Paper costs ten times as much as electronic storage.
- Do not just treat the symptoms; deal with the causes such as the proliferation of emails.
- Store back-up offsite.
- Know what documents to save, use retention schedules and destroy all not-needed documents.
- Use industry standard formats to enable migration and to ensure access to documents in the future.
- Do not focus on one area in isolation; it is more cost-effective to manage documents across the whole organization.

Chapter Six

Switching TRACs — Identifying the Dirt Roads

What we have been doing so far in this book is presenting an anecdotal or a story-based business case. We will be discussing in chapter eight how to develop your quantitative business case. However, it is important that you develop your own anecdotal business case. As any experienced sales professional will tell you every purchase decision is an emotional one. Basically any change in an organization requires selling ideas to get the funding to turn the ideas into action. Certainly, the rational argument is listened to but if you really want to overcome inertia and create momentum, tell a compelling story.

In making the decision to move forward with the ER-TRAC Framework we suggest you do some of the investigation we do. Before going to senior management or, if you are the CEO, before you raise this with your management team, it is a good idea to determine the potential for your organization.

You will be confident in presenting the ideas, have the anecdotal information collected and know where some of the information management challenges are.

Let's Walk Along Some of Those Dirt Roads

We find that all problems fall under one of these categories and sometimes in more than one category:

- information is difficult to retrieve, especially related information, which wastes time and does not always result in finding everything;
- sharing files results in wasting time looking for who has the file, lack of accountability for files or just walking across an office to get a file while a client is on hold;
- valuable space is wasted storing paper or servers fill up with disorganized and redundant information;
- concerns are raised about the security of files in the event of a disaster or disclosure or unauthorized access and destruction.
- access is needed from a remote location.

When we visit a potential client for the first time, we ask for a tour around the building as if we were new employees. As we walk through the various departments, we look and ask questions. So go off and see people. Call it developing interdepartmental rapport or say that you want to understand their business better. Your goal is to get a handle on what problems your organization has with records management. You will want to have a list of what business problems are being caused by information practices.

Implementing the ER-TRAC Framework takes commitment from senior management, through all levels of management and staff. Commitment will come when they understand what problems will be solved for them. We have seen CEOs skip this step and fail. We have had clients who do not want to bother senior management, who do not think all managers have to understand or who think that administrative assistants do not have to be involved in implementation. Remember that everyone in the organization has to use information and if you are seeking acceptance and accountability, it starts with letting people have a role in decisions that affect how they work. There is no other way to gain true corporate peace of mind for yourself and your employees.

Too Many Filing Cabinets = No Room for People

So let's take that walk. Look around and take note of how crowded the office areas are. How many filing cabinets are there? Do you see more than expected? This means that employees have to deal with a lot of paper, but it also usually means that they have not been applying retention schedules to the records. A benefit of the ER-TRAC Framework is that it has a system that can solve the problem of lack of space for staff workstations. We have seen cases where an organization has not had to move out of a building because of the room created by imaging records and managing all new records electronically.

What Fewer Filing Cabinets Might Mean

What if there are not many filing cabinets? We are running into this more and more. Employees are not printing off paper copies and they are keeping them electronically. Do they know that they do not have a proper record? An electronic record can only stand as evidence in court if it meets the requirements for documentary evidence and is part of a managed record system.

Central File Room Means Sharing of Files

When we see records filed centrally in a room, we know there is a frustrated clerk responsible for this room. There will be people who do not follow the procedures for taking out records, who do not respect the timelines for getting them back, who pass along the files to other people, who leave the files somewhere else and who misplace them on their desk or on top of their bookcases. It all adds up to many problems from having to share records when there is only one paper copy. In the electronic world, it is easy to keep a master copy safe while allowing access to those who are authorized.

We also look for people on telephones. Who are they talking to and do they need access to files while on the phone? We once implemented a system in a financing office where none of the business was walk-in. All business was conducted over the phone or by fax. With the new system, any agent could handle a call immediately because the files were all accessible through the system. Think of the savings in time and frustration for each customer and for each staff member.

What about computers? Of course, in most offices now, everyone works at a computer. It is interesting to note how people are grouped and what they are working on. When people are working on the same function they likely share electronic documents. What happens when someone is off work that day? Can he/she find his/her documents in the directory system? What about version control? When you have more than one person working on a document, such as reports, does everyone know which electronic copy is the final version? Do they know for sure that they have a paper copy of the final version? Do they ever change each other's electronic documents and mess them up for the creator?

Offsite Staff

Are all the employees located in this central location? Are they connected through a network? Do they have staff or customers who want access to the records in the office? In Alberta, the steel manufacturing industry has a requirement for turning over documents at the time of shipping. This creates a demand for immediate retrieval of many documents which can then be passed on. These documents are passed in binders of paper and the production of the binders is time-consuming and tedious. A product cannot normally be invoiced until it is shipped; production of these binders can delay shipping. This is a major problem requiring the fast retrieval and transmittal of all related information in an orderly fashion in order to keep the cash flowing in.

Privacy and Paper on Desks

Look at how much paper is sitting on the desks. Do employees have to refer to many files and do they have trouble finding all the files they need? Do they have a clean desk policy? Is privacy of information a challenge? Do they realize keeping information private is more convenient if they manage it electronically?

Human Resources

Ask how confident human resources personnel are that their private records like employee files, grievances and labour negotiations are protected. What are the implications if others, who do not have a right to see them, access these files? Do they know that if these files were managed in an ERMS they could secure access to the files? An ERMS will prevent unauthorized access ensuring that the original cannot be destroyed or edited.

If you want to find an example of records that are not printed, ask if all the current job descriptions are filed in paper format. Proof of compulsory training is an important record for employees. In the case of child welfare workers and related litigation, the question may be raised about whether the caseworker had taken training to recognize signs of sexual abuse. These records should have long retention periods and are often destroyed too soon.

Finance and Accounts Payable

Does the finance department pay auditors to look for records? Imaging systems have been justified based on the savings on auditor costs alone. Does finance retrieve invoices for other departments? How much better would it be if the departments could retrieve finance documents very quickly where and when they want to, and at the same time be unable to destroy, damage or take away the master copy? Does finance know that the general ledger is a permanent retention? Are the related records being stored to meet requirements for evidence? Are payroll records kept until the employee is seventy years old? How are they accessed and retrieved? Budget document from previous years are retrieved frequently and often for as long as fifteen years. Can the department find them when they need to?

Business Resumption

Has each department identified the records they would need for business resumption? Are those records backed up or could they even find them today?

Fleet Management

Do they have a complete history of maintenance to their fleet? If they can maintain a product history, on resale it could add $500 to $1,000 per vehicle. There could also be compliance questions if you are dealing with vehicles used for public transportation. Could they satisfy a judge that the vehicle involved in an accident was properly maintained?

Governance

What about records of enduring value, ones that mark milestones in the organization? Are these being stored in proper conditions? If these are still being accessed, how are they standing up? Did you know that things like sticky notes or just the oils on your fingers can hasten deterioration of the paper?

Have managers ensured back-up of vital records like this year's minutes or active client and donor lists? Is there a need to search the text of minutes and bylaws? An ERMS solution will give them the tools to do just that. Is correspondence and contract tracking an issue? This is a universal problem. There are even very specialized applications within enterprise content management suites that deal with this alone. Can managers access legal opinions they have been given? Do they know how important it is that these are handled as records so they do not lose their status as opinions? Do they travel and want to access records from wherever they are? Any business person who has traveled knows that you can become burdened with even more luggage if you have to take files.

Marketing

Does marketing have copies of all of their publications? Follow up this question with do they know when they were produced and who wrote them? Have they original electronic copies so they can reuse them? This is an area where they may have major version control problems. Electronic documents used in marketing have many versions and are frequently repurposed. It is important to accurately track these changes to be able to access and use each version appropriately. Marketing may also have concerns about finding information fast throughout the whole organization as they spearhead initiatives to react to the changing market environment.

Research

Do they know that research records have to be kept for a longer retention period than most business documents? How valuable would it be for them to know almost instantly what other research on this topic has been done in past years and perhaps in other parts of the organization? Are their copyright and trademark records safe and readily retrievable?

Sales

A big concern for sales departments are sales people who leave with client information. Ask how reassuring it would be for the sales department to know who accesses and copies records. Sales will also have the same needs as marketing with version control and repurposing of documents such as proposals. Ask how important it is that a sales professional is working from the right version of a price list. I heard the story of a financial company who had three different interest rates floating around the office during the retirement investment season. Ask about customer service complaints. How many of these are related to delays that could be solved by an ERMS?

Production/Operations

Compliance to regulatory requirements is important in the production and operations departments. The ISO Standard 9001 has 18 references to records keeping alone. It would be well-worth your while to read any applicable standards or legislation to determine what records requirements apply to them. If this is an ISO-certified company, they may be very receptive to learning about the ISO standard on Records Management ISO 15489-1 and ISO/TR 15489-2. Can they swiftly retrieve safety procedures? The quick search features of an ERMS system could be very useful here.

Ask about business resumption plans and if production/ operations has key records backed up.

Facilities and Properties

Drawings are needed as long as the organization has the building. Are these backed up yet accessible? Are contracts and change orders stored securely? There can be substantial costs if the organization cannot prove warranty claims. One organization had building files stored in a basement that leaked. Someone threw them out because they were wet. The files would have supported the case against the contractor, who was at fault for the leakage.

Next Steps

You may not want to take your initial investigation to this level of detail. You may have staff to assist you or you may want to hire a consultant. At least you will have an idea of some of the issues. In fact, you are on your way in performing the gap analysis that we will talk about in chapter nine.

You or your staff may want to start talking to vendors of enterprise content management solutions. We recommend this guardedly. You do not want to be swept into purchase decisions too early and then be locked in. On the positive side, you will get an idea of how the technologies work and how they make information more accessible. The vendors can also give you questions to ask of the information technology department and let you know what technical challenges there may be in implementation.

Initially you may only ask for support for developing the strategic plan for rolling out the ER-TRAC Framework or you may try for funding for the whole project. It really depends on management preferences.

All change management and project management textbooks talk about the importance of senior management support. We have found out the hard way that this is very true. It is important not to shy away from possible negative thinkers in management. Be persistent in finding a legitimate argument to persuade them. You may want to proceed to the planning stage even without their support so you will have more of the answers and a specific cost benefit analysis. In the next chapters we outline building the business case and how to structure your implementation approach.

ER-TRAC Tips

- Walk around the organization and talk to employees to identify their information management problems.
- Look for specific problems such as too many or too few filing cabinets, a central file room, sharing of documents, and privacy concerns.
- Look at problems specific to each department.
- Start where there is the most pain with support from those whose problems implementing the ER-TRAC Framework will be solved.

Chapter Seven

ER-TRAC Framework — Up Close

It costs ten times as much to manage information on paper as it does to manage information electronically. And when you manage information electronically we guess you will have about one hundred times more benefits.

As mentioned in chapter one, the first time we went to write this book we struggled with the need to label what we were recommending because it takes policy, processes, procedures, training and technology to implement our vision. So we developed a framework to help you see what we are talking about in this book. The ER-TRAC Framework pulls together all the elements required to yield the benefits that we describe in this book. ER-TRAC is a theoretical framework, not a product that you would purchase. It simply shows the elements of our solution that will lead to specific benefits.

What we have addressed in developing our ER-TRAC Framework and the resulting ER-TRAC Process (see Appendix A) is how to get organizations to the goal of electronic information management while recognizing that paper is good for reading and provides portability in small volumes. The main barrier to eliminating paper has been that most people find that reading a screen is slower than and not as comfortable as reading paper. The new LCD monitors have made a big improvement in readability but there is a ways to go before the monitor will replace paper.

Paper for reading will be around for some time yet. So let's accept that and move on to focusing on the difference between keeping paper around for reading purposes and keeping it for the information it contains. When you are finished with the paper, destroy it as it will be backed up electronically and accessible for printing again if need be.

This chapter goes into what we consider the necessary elements that must be in place to achieve the benefits we have been talking about.

Employee Accountability

Employees, including all executives and managers, have a duty to create records of their business transactions. Often we are asked what business transactions are. Basically they are decisions or milestones or communications of significance related to your business. That may not sound specific enough. A specific answer takes research and can be captured in what we call a records matrix, which will be discussed later in this chapter.

The main idea is that employees have to be held accountable for records just as they would be for the products or services they deliver and the other corporate assets that they are accountable for. A policy may be in place but we seldom find that employees are really held accountable for the records. We were involved in a situation where there were questions on how a purchasing agent chose one vendor over another. Management asked the agent to produce the records. He said that he had taken them home and his wife had thrown them out while cleaning. While this sounded all too convenient, management did not take action. It is not enough to have policy in place; management has to internalize the importance of records management. This comes through training, experience and leadership from senior management.

Employees should create only the records they have to, and keep them as long as they are needed and no more. Creating unnecessary records produces an unreasonable expectation that the records were required in the day-to-day course of operations and implies that other documents should have been created. In other words, holes appear to exist in the documentary trail. This creates expectations that may jeopardize the legal position of the organization in the event of litigation. In addition, the creation and management of unnecessary records can substantially add to the bottom line.

Employees have the duty to ensure they record information in a professional and ethical manner with the understanding that anything they record may be subject to scrutiny in a legal process. Even in these times, we see correspondence with obscenities in it.

In addition to ensuring employee accountability records have to be managed so they can be produced to prove legal and fiduciary responsibility. This will also result in a more efficient organization which provides excellent customer service. In short, organizations must establish records management programs.

The starting point for employee accountability and the creation of a records program is to create policy. It is amazing how few organizations have a policy that identifies records as being corporate property. We struggle constantly with the notion that records are an employee's property. Employees must recognize that after they are gone the organization may be held accountable for the work they did. Records give the organization valuable information about the nature and content of current and past work.

The best guideline for developing a policy on records that we have seen is the ISO standard on Records Management ISO 15489-1 and ISO/TR 15489-2. Regardless of how complete the policy is, management needs to provide leadership to ensure that employees understand and follow the policy in everyday activities.

You can see that employee accountability is one of the key policies in the framework on the next page. Let us look at how the other policy and tools work to provide your organization with the full benefits of this solution.

ER-TRAC™ Framework		
Fast TRAC to the high performance workplace		
Policy	**Tools**	
• Employee Accountability	• Enterprise Content Management Software	• Records Creation Matrix
• Electronic Record Master and Paper Transitory	• Corporate Taxonomy	• Information Security Matrix
• Policy & Procedures for Electronic Records as Documentary Evidence	• Retention & Disposition Schedule	• Change Management Plan
Benefits		
• Corporate Peace of Mind	• Compliance Assurance	
• Improved Customer Service	• Increased Security	
• Efficient Processes	• Business Resumption	

Electronic Master Record

The ER-TRAC Framework stipulates that every electronic information management system be implemented to meet the requirements for electronic records as documentary evidence. This includes databases and enterprise resource systems.

For an electronic record to be a master record, it must meet the requirements for electronic records as documentary evidence. By master record, we mean the one that is considered the reliable one, the one that is the last to be destroyed or the one that will be kept permanently. Everything else is a copy. In the paper world, it is referred to as the original.

Paper-Transitory Record

Paper is expensive to manage. As we have said at the start of the chapter, we have calculated paper to be about ten times as expensive to manage as electronic records. It is expensive to copy and to process. It is a great medium for reading. In small quantities, it is easy to carry and consult. Once paper has served its purpose, staff should destroy it.

Electronic Records as Documentary Evidence

There is now strong legislative support that recognizes electronic records as documentary evidence. The legislation does not say how electronic records are to be managed, only that they are legal when managed "within a system." The legislation anticipates the use of standards to guide the management of electronic records.

The same principles of records management that apply to paper still apply to electronic records such as the need for trustworthy, authentic records. The standards require that a manual be prepared which outlines how the electronic records are managed within the organization. This manual can be taken to court to demonstrate evidentiary integrity.

As part of our practice we develop a manual for our clients containing all the relevant policies and procedures.

There are a number of requirements for electronic records as documentary evidence, which we will not go into in this book. They are not burdensome and generally constitute good management detail. However, it is important to know a couple of things that are related. It is not all about technology; you must have the policy and procedures in place. The technology is important for securing the records and for keeping an audit trail of who accesses the records. The need for the audit trail creates the need for the purchase of an electronic records management system. We routinely implement systems ensuring that these requirements are addressed.

Enterprise Content Management (ECM) Software

The key applications listed below comprise what is generally known as ECM software:

- electronic document management/electronic records management/imaging, which we refer to in this book as an ERMS;
- business process management software: if all your information is digital, why would you need to print it to handle it? In our framework, we see automated business processes as a key to achieving all the benefits from managing information electronically;
- search engines that will search all digital repositories of information within your organization or will move out to search the Internet; and
- web content management.

It is not our intention in this book to go into these technologies. If you want to learn more about them, we encourage you to go to Association for Information and Image Management (AIIM) website at www.aiim.org.

As you can see in our framework, technology is only part of the solution. It is only one tool. Successful implementation will take into consideration all the policy elements and tools of our ER-TRAC Framework.

Corporate Taxonomy

A consistent classification system (taxonomy) for the whole organization needs to be developed. To retrieve information there has to be consistency in how it is organized and how it is described. The corporate taxonomy is developed using the preferred terms of the organization. The system is based on the functions of the organization and not on the organizational structure. Structure changes frequently and functions tend not to. The corporate taxonomy is a living system that needs a custodian to tend to it. In the ER-TRAC Framework, corporate taxonomy needs to become pervasive in all information management systems.

Records Retention and Disposition Schedule

The records retention and disposition schedule is approved by the policy body of an organization to specify how long information should be kept and what its final disposition will be — destruction or transfer to an archival authority. This schedule governs what information can be destroyed and it is not dependent on what any individual employee wants or thinks is necessary. The retention and disposition schedule is developed based on a review of the legislative and regulatory environment, professional standards and business needs.

If you ask most business professionals how long they need to keep records they will come up with seven years. This is a typical requirement for financial records but other records may vary. Under environmental legislation, there can be requirements of twenty-five years or longer.

We visited a municipality where they had a room full of records they wanted cleaned up. They sent in a summer student with little direction. They discovered sometime after that the student had thrown out the City Charter. A precious document in the city's history was lost. Managing records requires expertise, and a records management program should be implemented in any business with the same level of care as finance and human resource programs.

Records Creation Matrix

This is a term and practice that we have developed. This tool documents what records an organization is obligated to create to meet regulatory or legislative requirements or to comply with good business practices. The development of a records matrix will assist your organization in identifying what is created and paring it down to what must be created.

The first step in developing a records matrix is to identify which records your organization is required to create. In order to build the matrix numerous factors must be taken into consideration such as, but not limited, to the following:

- legislative and regulatory requirements;
- corporate policy and procedures;
- organization's business processes;
- organization's position specific requirements;
- industry practice; and

- professional or association code of conduct requirements.

Often, new employees do not know what records to create to protect the organization. In addition, they may not have a clue about what they should not create to protect the organization.

We believe that the requirements to create, capture or generate records should be imbedded in the organization's job descriptions. The records matrix will facilitate this task. The requirement to create records should also be imbedded in the policies of the organization. Organizations should communicate and emphasize to its personnel the importance of creating only those records for which a need has been identified. When in doubt, personnel review the records matrix for guidance.

Information Security Matrix

The information security matrix allocates who can have what level of access to information in the organization. It applies not just to documents but also to all information repositories, such as databases, videos and photos.

The implementation of electronic records management systems has created the need for security matrixes. Electronic records are stored in a secure central repository on the network. The security built into the system controls who can access which records and what rights they have to change or destroy the records. It has to be developed to ensure that it protects the best interests of the organization and meet any legislative or regulatory requirements such as in-privacy legislation and proprietary information.

We have chosen to use a matrix approach to ensure consistency and ensure that there are no orphaned records. The matrix is developed along the functional lines of the organization. We have found that the security matrix document is useful for guiding access decisions to all information holdings in organizations including paper files and databases.

Change Management Plan

Whatever you put in place, whether it is policy, technology or records management tools, it means nothing if people do not use it. We have found that the simplest approach is to involve as many staff as possible at all stages and to ensure that a vision is developed that provides benefits for everyone. Here is a sample of a vision statement:

> All corporate employees will have access to corporate records required to perform their duties, independent of geography, time and original format of the records.

A statement like this is not enough in itself. We like to work with each department on developing its business case. The secret of success in acceptance is finding a business problem that can be solved with the implementation of the ER-TRAC Framework. There is more on how to identify those problems in chapters six and eight.

We believe in having a planned approach to change management but we are not tied to any set methodology. We find that organizations have come to realize the importance of change management and have a methodology or expertise that they use. It is very important to have the key players in the organization help to prepare a plan on how to manage the change along with the other steps in the project. However, there is no substitute for management showing enthusiasm and walking the talk.

ER-TRAC Tips

- Every electronic information management system must be implemented to meet the requirements for records as documentary evidence.
- You need to have documented policies and procedures and a good system of records management to support an ERMS.
- The technology is important to secure records and to create an audit trail.
- In addition to ECM software, the ER-TRAC Framework tools are the records creation matrix, corporate taxonomy, information security matrix, retention and disposition schedules and change management

Chapter Eight

ER-TRAC — Off the Paper Trails onto the Highway

Are you ready to start down the road to implementing our ER-TRAC Framework? In this chapter, we cover the highlights of implementation from our ER-TRAC Process (see Appendix A). We find most people think this process could take years. Not so — the technology is affordable and tested. The greatest challenge is giving the process the time and commitment it requires and ensuring that corporate leaders provide the motivation. With effective leadership, the organization will achieve the paybacks.

We have developed a process that starts with working with those persons in an organization who are interested in pursuing improvements from information management to implementation and maintenance. Not every aspect of this framework has to be implemented at once. It is important to set up the policy initially but implementation of the components of enterprise content management is best if they are staged. For example you might want to start with document management and imaging and leave workflow, which automates your processes, to a later implementation. You could start the other way around by automating your business processes. The priorities can be identified in the needs analysis in the planning phase.

The six stages are of the ER-TRAC Process are:

- discovery;
- executive/corporate support and funding;
- planning;
- design;
- implementation; and
- maintenance.

Within each of these stages, we address five areas or organizational functions:

- operations;
- legal;
- technology;
- records management; and
- human resources.

A chart of this approach is available from us by emailing us at trac@tracrecords.ca or visiting our website at www.tracrecords.ca.

Discovery

The discovery stage is the process we described in Chapter Six where you consider what problems staff may be having with management of information. Have a look at the software currently in use, find out who is interested and what the showstoppers might be.

Executive/Corporate Support and Funding

As we mentioned, initially you may want to only ask for support for developing the strategic plan for implementing the ER-TRAC Framework or you may try for funding for the whole project. It really depends on management preferences.

What is critical here is that you have involved senior management fully. The implementation is going to require leadership from them and the sooner you focus their attention on the problems that the ER-TRAC Framework and Process will address the better. This is where you can use the information from your walk-about. We have found that senior management is more interested in the problems that the solution will address for their staff rather than any general corporate concerns or accountability to stakeholders. The more specific you can be for each department the better.

This ER-TRAC Framework does involve working in a different way, where paper is optional. We find that change management is best achieved by involving as many staff as possible in the process. More than anything they have to digest what is coming. Often decision-makers shy away from conflict by keeping plans under wraps and then springing them on the staff. Few people can handle being surprised and everyone likes to be asked for their opinion and help when it counts.

We have often found those hardest to convince become the staunchest supporters in the end. It is best to get any challenges dealt with as early possible before any big bucks are spent. They may identify some problems that can be readily addressed at the planning stage that will not be so easily incorporated when money has been spent on the implementation. As we said earlier, pick a framework for change management and have a strategy as you move throughout your implementation.

Planning Including Gap Analysis

You do not want to start by buying enterprise content management, electronic records, imaging, or electronic document management software. The time for that will be when you have the plan finished. Software is a tool not a solution. You have to know what problems you need to solve, where you are going and how you want to proceed. Begin with the end in mind. That is why we start with a plan. Our strategic plan starts with the gap analysis. This identifies what you need to implement the ER-TRAC Framework in the five areas or functions: operations, legal, technology, records management and human resources (see Appendix C for more information on gap analysis). Not to be forgotten are the other applications in the IT environment which should be evaluated. We evaluate these systems and make sure that anything that could be considered a record is managed as one and is able to meet the requirements for electronic records as documentary evidence.

We identify where the organization is at in these areas today. We then apply the legislation, standards and regulations that affect the organization, put them within the context of the organization's vision, direction and requirements, and setup an analytical framework. From there we identify the gaps and base planning on filling those gaps.

We are often asked to do a current cost analysis. This is a way for organizations to determine, often for the first time, the current cost of managing their information. This can be compared directly to the costs of the new solution and the anticipated hard benefits that will result (see Appendix B for more information on cost analysis).

Before implementing any software, you need to ensure that your organization has an up-to-date taxonomy and a retention and disposition schedule with legal and board approval. We often develop or update these for our clients. We also develop a security matrix which shows who will have what level of access to information. The security access for all electronic applications and paper systems must be consistent. In addition, it is essential that there is an up-to-date, legally admissible policy and procedures manual.

To meet legal requirements electronic records must be able to be used as documentary evidence and must meet compliance and regulatory obligations. We recommend including your corporate lawyers throughout this project.

Design

Once the strategic plan is completed, we refer you again to AIIM at www.aiim.org. AIIM has a big trade show every spring and it has all kinds of guides and standards to assist you. A useful organization for assistance on records management is ARMA International at www.arma.org. There are other organizations that can be assistance also, such as the e-Content Institute at www.econtentinstitute.org.

The time has come to address the purchase of the software. You may want to hire consultants. It is important for your key information management staff to develop an understanding of the technology and be involved in the process. You will need to know the hardware requirements for the software that you will be buying. We often start with electronic document management and/or electronic records software depending on the business needs and the software suite. Workflow is next. Web content depends on how extensive your website is and what problems you are having maintaining it. We identify the value of each product to your organization before recommending it and work with you to set the priorities for implementation.

The enterprise content management field has matured and there are a number of excellent products to work with. Do not get so focused on product that you do not consider who will work with you on the integration of the system and provide the support you require after implementation.

Implementation

Start where there is the Most Pain

You start where there is the most pain or where there may be the most support for implementation of the ER-TRAC Framework. Then you can roll out to the rest of the organization. We believe there is a certain amount of learning that has to happen before you implement a new system throughout the whole organization.

Involve as Many of your Staff as Possible

You may need help from outside expertise, depending on the skills and knowledge in your company. Nevertheless, it is still a good idea to include staff members on the team. You will have already included staff at all stages of the process, and it is important to continue to include them during implementation. We believe that the more your staff under-stands the problems to be solved and the expected outcomes and benefits of the process, the more accepting of the change they will be.

Staff training is essential to the success of any new system. Training is not just the transfer of technical knowledge so that that the new electronic information system can be used. A policy and procedures manual must be developed and staff trained in their accountability and responsibilities to successfully manage corporate information.

Maintenance

After implementation, there should be well trained staff, a completed policy and procedures manual that will support the legality of electronic documents and a clear plan for maintaining the system. It is not over when the framework is implemented. It is important to understand that for the ER-TRAC Framework to be successful you need to maintain the policies, procedures, processes and technology that you developed for it. It is also important to evaluate the success of the solution and make small adaptations as necessary.

ER-TRAC Tips

- The ER-TRAC Process has six stages: discovery, executive/corporate support and funding, planning, design, implementation and maintenance.
- Within each stage there are five areas or functions to address: operations, legal, technology, records management and human resources.
- Don't start with the software start with the end in mind.
- Involve staff at every stage.
- Use a staged implementation starting where there is the most pain.

Chapter Nine

Destination — Corporate Peace of Mind

From Highway to Superhighway

Once an organization commits to the ER-TRAC Framework it will be in a position to leverage the business process management/workflow technology. This will enable it to radically change the way it creates, captures or generates information.

The basic principles behind records management will not disappear. Information will still be grouped by related subjects to enable efficient retrieval and disposition. What will change is that the business process will determine where and when information is captured, managed and retrieved. More importantly it will determine which information is kept and for how long.

The ER-TRAC Framework ensures that the employees who use the information are responsible for attaching the metadata to documents that are created, captured or generated in the ECM system.

The design of the business processes will ensure that the metadata required to file the documents will be imbedded in the process, thus eliminating this task. The pesky records management function of physically filing will be eliminated. Records created, captured or generated as part of the business process will be automatically filed as directed by the records matrix.

Workflow software will present to the users the forms or documents that need to be completed as part of their input into the process. Organizations will be able to enforce standardization of the format of documents, reports and forms and the users will have less and less control of the output. Compliance, due diligence and risk management will be built into the business processes.

In short, you will have "Fast TRACed" to the high performance workplace. However, the benefits of implementing the ER-TRAC Framework go beyond improved productivity to the very heart of your organization.

The Journey

We wrote this book to share what we have learned from working with many organizations on their information management problems. We have brought together our knowledge and experience in records management, information technology and corporate governance. We have sorted through the practices we use and have packaged our approach into the framework in a way that we think is fresh. The framework we have described in this book goes beyond solving information technology challenges to encourage you to question how your organization manages information. We hope this will motivate you to take action that will lead to corporate peace of mind.

What is peace of mind for most of us? Is it not the feeling of a job well done, having one's physical space free of clutter and in order, having a vision for where we are going, being free of baggage so we can be nimble and not wasting time doing what is tiring and tedious, feeling safe and secure, feeling open with no guilt, living honestly and being productive? Corporate peace of mind is based on the same principles. This book is about finding corporate peace of mind through improved information management practices.

Vision for Corporate Peace of Mind

Here is our vision of corporate peace of mind:

> Employees have easy access to the most current, correct information that they need to do their jobs. The information is accessible through a web browser wherever they need it, in the office, out in the field or across the world. Information is stored offsite in case of disaster recovery. Legal costs have been minimized.

Productive

> Whether employees are serving the public, clients in other businesses or their own internal customers, they can respond to requests quickly and confidently. They can tell customers where, when and how their requests are being handled.

Clutter-Free

Employees are clear on what information they need to save as records and what information should be in those records. They have the tools to store them easily. The only paper in the work areas is paper that can be disposed of when employees are finished reading it.

Automated Processes

Employees do not fill out paper forms. They use the automated business process that suits what they need to do. It keeps them advised on what is happening to their tasks.

Compliance

A compliance audit is announced and everyone says "ok, no sweat." They will show the auditors how to search for all the information. If the information is not there, they will know who is accountable and ask that person where it is.

Business Continuity

Management does not worry about what a disaster would do to their information holdings because they have everything backed up and stored offsite. They know that those who will take over their jobs will be able to access the information of today and use it.

Security

Management does not have to worry about unauthorized people accessing the information from within the company, as access to information will be determined and controlled. An audit trail will show who accessed the documents and what they did with it. Internal or external users will not see private information unless they have authorization.

Job Well-Done

All employees feel they have done their job well and go home with peace of mind.

Direct Pointing to the Heart of the Organization

When we were researching what peace of mind is, we came upon Zen philosophy. While we cannot claim to be experts on Zen philosophy, there were clearly elements of the Zen teachings that struck chords with us. Zen is defined in one book as "the direct pointing to the heart of man."[4] We envision that competently managed information is the direct pointing to the heart of the organization.

Corporate Liberation

Zen discusses how to live in the world and find liberation. We envision an organization's leadership living in a legalistic, competitive, corporate world. They will find liberation through having what they need to make their

---

[4]Bancroft, Anne. The Wisdom of Zen. Oneword Publications, 2001

business decisions and to meet their records obligations responsibly, even honourably, unfettered by excess information and time-consuming processes.

Zen uses concrete presentation rather than abstract. In this book, we provided a concrete framework for managing information rather than general abstraction. We also provided concrete examples of the benefits of following our framework.

Whether you relate best to our metaphor of moving from dirt roads to paved highways, or to finding corporate liberation in the Zen way, it is important for you to know that your goal is achievable. It will not happen overnight, but it can happen much faster than you think if you commit to it and plan for it. It may seem overwhelming at first and there may be difficult spots along the journey. We assure you that whenever we have helped corporate personnel organize and manage their information they not only improve their productivity, they gain control of their work and experience new levels of satisfaction. They even have peace of mind.

How to Contact the Authors

We are located in Sherwood Park, Alberta, Canada, next door to the city of Edmonton, Alberta. We would be pleased to answer any questions or receive your comments on the book. We are also available to work with organizations on implementing our framework and to speak at conferences.

TRAC Records Inc.   www.tracrecords.ca
#212, 10 Chippewa Road   www.patbeelby.com
Sherwood Park, AB T8A 3Y1   trac@tracrecords.ca
780-449-4240

To sign up for our free newsletter, *KeepTRAC*, visit our website www.tracrecords.ca

Appendix A

ER-TRAC Process Highlights

The Stages

1. During discovery, you identify the information management problems in your organization and assess the current ECM technology. You then identify and gain an understanding of organizational records practices and the general benefits your organization could gain by implementing the ER-TRAC Framework.

2. You get the organizational support and funding you need to move forward.

3. You integrate the strategic plan with your organization's vision and goals and evaluate using needs assessment and gap analysis to identify where there is the most need for change and to quantify the expected benefits.

4. You design a customized solution to meet your organization's business needs.

5. You use a staged approach to implementation to maximize benefits, transfer expertise to your staff and manage change.

6. You ensure there is a policy manual, scheduled reviews and trained staff to maintain your system.

The Keys to Success (Functional Areas)

The ER-TRAC Process ensures your success by focusing on benefits and operational problem solving. The ER-TRAC Process ensures employee accountability, training and change management. TRAC sees technology as a tool to leverage your information assets, not as an end in itself. TRAC assesses the technology you have and implements an integrated system using a master electronic record rather than a paper record.

A chart of this approach is available from us by emailing us at trac@tracrecords.ca or on our website at www.tracrecords.ca.

Appendix B

Identifying Current Costs and Cost-Benefit Analysis

Identifying current costs associated with the records and information management program is often a challenge. Costs associated with the records and information management program addresses, but is not limited to, the following:

- operation and business processes;
- financial management;
- personnel management;
- facilities and equipment;
- transaction costs;
- information management costs; and
- management overhead cost.

How TRAC can Help

TRAC's cost benefit analysis tool can assist in determining the return on investment of implementing new ECM technologies and will:

- calculate existing costs of a traditional paper system or an electronic system;
- compare the cost of conducting business one way versus another;
- create benchmarks of the records and information management operation as it is today;

- determine the cost effectiveness of switching from one technology to another (such as a paper-base to electronic document-based);
- evaluate an existing ERMS system to determine how to maximize benefits; and
- identify outsourcing options (such as using an Application Service Provider).

Go to our website at www.tracrecords.ca to download the brochure on Cost-Benefit Analysis or contact us at trac@tracrecords.ca.

Appendix C

Records and Information Management Gap Analysis

The purpose of the records and information management gap analysis is to determine the state of the Records and Information Management program when measured against industry best practices. A secondary purpose is to identify the overall vision of the Records and Information Management program and identify the gap between the existing program and the desired outcome.

The gap analysis is usually conducted as follows:

- interviews with management team;
- interviews with centralized program area i.e. finance, human resources, etc.;
- interview with specific program areas; and
- review of findings with management team.

Vision

The first step is to develop a vision for the Records and Information Management program. Included in the vision can be the future state of the Records and Information Management program. For example, designate the electronic record as the master record of the organization.

Organization Information

Organization information is gathered on, but not limited to, the following areas:

- accountability in the areas of information management policy, legislative and regulatory environment, records retention schedule, privacy legislation and procedures;
- records generation and volume;
- records organization classification plans;
- records maintenance;
- file control including retention and disposition.
- forms program;
- training records personnel, management and users; and
- records security and protection.

For more information, contact TRAC at trac@tracrecords.ca